True Tales
of
Adventurers
& Explorers

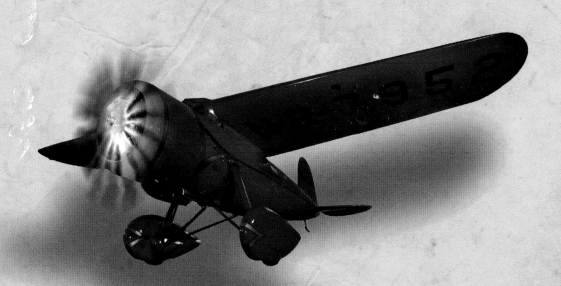

Credits

Editors: Claire Boulter, Anna Hall, Paul Jordin, Holly Poynton and Rebecca Tate

Consultant: Rachel Clark

With thanks to Rachel Grocott, Holly Poynton, Karen Wells, Janet Berkeley, Alison Griffin, Judy Hornigold and Lucy Towle for the proofreading.

With thanks to Laura Jakubowski for the copyright research.

With thanks to John Kitching for the design work.

Published by CGP

ISBN: 978 1 84762 476 5

Printed by Elanders Ltd, Newcastle upon Tyne.

The chapters in this book are based on real people and real events. However, some situations and dialogue have been changed for dramatic purposes. Some minor characters have been invented; any similarity to a real person, living or dead, is purely coincidence.

Contents

Acknowledgements

Image on cover and introduction page by Eric Long, National Air and Space Museum, Smithsonian Institution

Background image on cover © iStockphoto.com/Trifonov_Evgeniy

Image on page 7: A Turkish Bazaar, 1867. Private Collection / Photo © Christie's Images / Bridgeman Images

Image on page 11: Emperor Wu leaving his palace. © Archives Charmet / Bridgeman Images

Image of Kuruman mission station on page 17 by Andrew Hall, licensed for re-use under the creative commons licence http://creativecommons.org/licenses/by-sa/3.0/deed.en

Image of David Livingstone on back cover, contents page and page 24 © Pictorial Press Ltd / Alamy

Image on back cover, contents page and page 27: Portrait of Nellie Bly, c.1888

Image on page 27: Pittsburgh 1874 Otto Krebs

Image on page 28: Nelly Bly, with variations, Firth, Pond and Co., New York, 1853, monographic. Library of Congress, Music Division

Image on page 30: Printing House Square 1868 Lith. W. C. Rogers & Co. For Jos. Shannons's Manual 1868

Image of rat on page 31: © Ilya Stcherbakov/iStock/Thinkstock

Image of money on page 32: © Jupiterimages/liquidlibrary/Thinkstock

Image of book cover on page 33: © Chris Howes/Wild Places Photography / Alamy

Image of truck on page 42 by Lglswe, licensed for re-use under the creative commons licence http://creativecommons.org/licenses/by-sa/3.0/deed.en

Image on page 43: Amelia Earhart and Neta Snook: George Palmer Putnam Collection of Amelia Earhart Papers, Courtesy of Purdue University Libraries, Karnes Archives & Special Collections.

Image of Amelia Earhart on page 45: © Pictorial Press Ltd / Alamy

Image of female pilots on page 46: WASP Pilots in front of USAAF B-17 "Pistol Packin Mama." (U.S. Air Force photo)

Image of Amelia Earhart on back cover, contents page and page 47 © Pictorial Press Ltd / Alamy

Image of Purdue University on page 48: Diego Delso, Wikimedia Commons, CC-BY-SA

With thanks to Alamy, CGTextures.com, Clipart.com, iStockphoto.com, Look and Learn, CorbisImages.com, Mary Evans Picture Library and Thinkstockphotos.co.uk for permission to use the stock images in this book.

Amelia Earhart™ is a trademark of Amy Kleppner, as heir to the Estate of Muriel Morrissey. www.AmeliaEarhart.com

Zhang Qian

"Father of the Silk Road"

written by Anna Hall

FEBRUARY 139 BC Enthroned on a lofty pedestal, Emperor Wu radiated a calm authority that silenced the entire room.

"Gentlemen." His voice boomed out around the high-ceilinged hall, bouncing off the walls and returning as a faint echo. "For too long, we have been plagued by the barbaric Xiongnu (She-ong-new) people. They have ravaged our trade routes and hounded us with savage raids. The time has come to take action."

There were murmurs of excitement from around the hall. What was the Emperor about to suggest?

"I propose sending an **ambassador** to form an **alliance** with the Yuezhi (You-way-juh) tribe. They too have been tormented by the brutal Xiongnu, but if we join forces, we may be strong enough to defeat them. If there is a soul in this room brave enough to undertake this treacherous voyage across hostile Xiongnu territory to reach the Yuezhi, let him speak now."

Over 2000 years ago, Emperor Wu ruled the Han Empire, an area that covered a large part of modern-day China. During his reign, the Han Empire was under constant threat from the ruthless Xiongnu tribe, who occupied the territory to the north of the Han Empire.

The high-ranking officials shifted awkwardly in their chairs and fixed their eyes on the ground as Emperor Wu's gaze swept around the hall. His piercing stare reached into every corner of the room. There was no escape. Suddenly there was a sharp intake of breath as a wise-looking man with several coloured ribbons decorating his chest stood up. He made a low and elegant bow before beginning to speak.

"Your Excellency, what about Zhang Qian (Jang Chee-an)? He is a young man of great strength and determination. His generosity and warmth are famous throughout the court. He would make an excellent ambassador for the Han Dynasty."

A Daunting Mission

MAY 138 BC Zhang Qian peered up at the towering stone gates, beyond which lay the path that would take him away from the safety of the Han capital, Chang'an. He held aloft a slender bamboo stick decorated with tufts of ox hair that had been given to him by the Emperor. It was a symbol of his status as a Royal Ambassador of Han.

Behind him, over one hundred men from all walks of life waited for their orders. Each man, from the soldiers and officers down to the lowly **porters**, had abandoned his comfortable life to set off on a treacherous journey into the unknown, with Zhang Qian at the helm.

At Zhang's side was Ganfu, a loyal servant of the Han Dynasty and a skilled archer. They exchanged a brief glance, their eyes concealing a flicker of excitement behind their calm, warrior-like glaze. Zhang gave a tiny nod and then turned to his men, distributing a scroll to each recruit.

Briefing: Mission to Yuezhi

We will be travelling for many miles through hostile territory to reach the Yuezhi. The following instructions will help to ensure your survival:

Throughout the mission:

- *Follow the route you have been given unless otherwise instructed.*

- *Be sparing with your food and water.*

- *Do not overfeed your camels. They are naturally very strong and do not require much food or water.*

- *Aim for an average speed of 3 miles per hour and a distance of 25 miles per day.*

- *Remember, you are representing the Empire, often in unfamiliar territory. Behave with dignity and honour.*

Once we have entered Xiongnu territory:

- *Try to make as little noise as possible.*

- *Conceal yourselves by day.*

- *Travel only under the cover of night.*

Zhang and his men planned to follow the route shown, travelling north-west from Chang'an.

A Catastrophic Encounter

THREE MONTHS LATER Zhang and his men were making their way through the treacherous sands of the Taklamakan (Tak-la-ma-kan) Desert. Nobody spoke as they trudged on, weary from thirst and the heat. They had seen countless dunes and thousands of stars but not a single other person.

Suddenly, Ganfu interrupted the eerie silence with a sharp intake of breath. He gestured frantically at the glimmer of a reflection on the horizon. "The Xiongnu have come for us!" he cried in horror. "We're done for!"

Zhang Qian's route took him west around the edge of the Taklamakan Desert, one of the harshest environments in the world. Locals refer to it as the 'Land of Death'.

Determined not to reveal his fear, Zhang drew his sword and addressed his men: "Gentlemen, we shall soon find ourselves under attack. We shall fight courageously and stand together against these barbaric tribesmen. Some may fall, but we will endure this peril with brave hearts. We shall remain the loyal forces of Emperor Wu."

Within minutes, swarms of men on horses were charging towards them, their arrows raining down in front of Zhang's men. Seconds later, the attackers were upon them, wielding swords and spears and screaming blood-curdling battle cries. Beneath their helmets, the men's faces were covered in jagged scars. Zhang's men fought courageously, but they were outnumbered by the ferocious Xiongnu warriors.

Zhang felt a huge hand roughly grasp the back of his neck, and a sack was thrown over his head. He gasped for breath in the suffocating darkness as his hands were bound. Zhang trembled with terror, and yet he couldn't help feeling a small tingle of relief. If the men were going to the trouble of binding and blindfolding him, it was unlikely that they would kill him straight away. Instead, he suspected he would be taken to the Chanyu (Chan-you), the ruler of the Xiongnu, who would decide his fate.

A traveller today in the Taklamakan Desert

Clipped Wings

AUGUST 134 BC As the evening light began to fade, Zhang shouldered his pack and began the long trek back to his tent. How the mighty had fallen! He had left Chang'an as a royal **dignitary**, gloriously attired in silk robes. Now he was reduced to a lowly shepherd, forced to wear simple trousers fashioned from itchy cloth.

Whilst he was enslaved, Zhang managed to earn the respect of the Chanyu. As a result, he was allowed some freedom and was even given a Xiongnu woman as a wife.

The Xiongnu had been impressed by Zhang's bravery during their attack, so they had allowed him to live. He had been sold in a slave auction to a rich **aristocrat**, who worked him to the bone. By day, Zhang traipsed over the mountains fulfilling his duties as a shepherd. By night, he transformed into a household slave.

Back in his tent, he pulled his journal from its secret hiding place. He was completely exhausted, but he summoned all the energy he could and began to write.

14th August, Year 7 of Emperor Wu's reign

I must begin with an apology — I have neglected this journal for far too long. I return to it today on the fourth anniversary of my capture by the Xiongnu.

Life here in the mountains is a constant trial. Today, I awoke at 4 am. I left my beautiful wife and my precious son and headed out to herd the flocks of cows and sheep. As usual, my first task was to check that none of the flock were lame. When I counted the sheep, I realised that two were missing. I spent the rest of the morning searching high and low for them, eventually finding them sheltering under a juniper tree about a mile away. The rest of the day was taken up with finding water and new pastures for the animals.

Now I am back in my tent. I have managed to snatch a few moments to write this, but soon I will have to go and cook for my master. After that, I will have to clean his tent. If I am lucky, I might catch a glimpse of Ganfu on my way home.

I remain determined to complete my mission. Whenever I feel I am losing my resolve, I need only seek out my most treasured possession — the bamboo token given to me by the Emperor as I was leaving Chang'an. Every night I pray that one day I will be able to continue my journey. Until then, I remain the loyal servant of Emperor Wu.

A Slave Unchained

MAY 128 BC Perched on a rock near his flock, Zhang tried to stop himself from fidgeting. He could feel an ice-cold trickle of sweat making its way down his left cheek. Fixing his eyes on the sprawling camp below, Zhang attempted to focus his mind on the task ahead. From this distance the camp looked like a toy town, with little pin-prick fires glowing dimly through the misty half-light of the breaking dawn.

Zhang had spent the past few months gradually moving his flock further and further away from the camp. His current position was near the top of the mountain and behind a rocky outcrop; no one would notice his absence until late that evening.

His palms were clammy and his breath came in short sharp bursts. It was now or never. All he had to do was wait for his wife and son to arrive with Ganfu and then they could resume their long trek to the Yuezhi.

The rattle of dislodged pebbles caught his attention, and as he peered over the cliff edge, he spotted Ganfu scrambling purposefully up the concealed side of the mountain, Zhang's wife and son trailing behind him. The mountain was steep and rocky, making the climb a strenuous task, but all three of the climbers were determined. Willpower alone would propel them up the mountain and onwards to face the journey ahead.

"You made it!" cried Zhang, his eyes flitting from left to right, scanning the horizon for any sign that they had been spotted. "Now we can begin."

The four travellers turned their backs on camp below and took their first steps towards freedom. They were no longer slaves. They were intrepid **pioneers**, questing through the desolate wilderness.

The Xiongnu territory was located north of the Gobi Desert.

A Force of Nature

A WEEK LATER The four travellers were still making their way across the barren desert to the Yuezhi. As the suffocating midday heat reached its peak, the sky began an ominous transformation from vivid blue to an angry shade of crimson. An unnerving stillness crept through the dunes.

Quietly at first, a strange whistling sound reached their ears. Then it became a thunderous roar. The group exchanged glances, paralysed by the thought of what was approaching. Huge, billowing clouds of sand appeared on the horizon, ambushing them just as the Xiongnu had done. The wall of sand hit Zhang and the others with a supernatural force, knocking them to the ground. Sand whipped at their faces, lashed their flesh and tore at their clothes. It was everywhere. They were breathing it in and spitting it out, tasting the bitter grit in their mouths. The pain was almost unbearable.

Zhang shielded his eyes with his hand and strained to see through the whirling sand. He could just make out the hunched figures of his wife and son. Desperately, he crawled towards them. Summoning his last shred of strength, he threw his body over their fragile frames to shield them. Just as Zhang began to feel himself slipping out of consciousness, the storm's intensity lessened and the sun shimmered through the drifts of settling sand.

Zhang pulled himself into a sitting position. Rubbing sand from his eyes, he spoke hoarsely. "We must find shelter. We will not survive another storm like that."

"We are just a few days from the safety of Dayuan (Da-you-an)," Ganfu responded, fighting to regain control of his breathing. "I have heard rumours of huge fortified towns hidden between the dunes there."

The group gathered their meagre belongings. Calling on their last reserves of energy, they trudged on.

Zhang's journey took him through the snow-capped Pamir Mountains.

A Celestial Sighting

JUNE 128 BC The party staggered into a walled city in Dayuan (a country to the west of modern-day China). They fell to their knees in front of a small well and lapped greedily at handfuls of warm water. Once refreshed, the group wandered along dusty roads and down narrow alleyways, heading deeper into the heart of the city. Sounds drifted towards them: the excited clamour of a crowd and, now and again, a faint strain of music.

They emerged in the midst of a chaotic market scene. The air was a stifling cocktail of dust and sweat, and yet the alluring smells of rich foods and exotic spices managed to pierce their way through. The whole spectacle was awash with colour, from the women's sparkling earrings, brooches and bracelets to the men's lavish turbans. The spices were arranged in a patchwork of intense shades, whilst tables of gleaming gems, ornate scrolls and intricate metalwork glittered in the sun. People rushed past carrying rolled carpets and giant urns; men pushing heavy wooden handcarts weaved in and out of the crowd, skirting ankles and elbows at great speed. Zhang had been to the markets of Chang'an, but he had never witnessed anything like this.

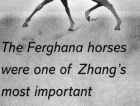

The Ferghana horses were one of Zhang's most important discoveries. They came to be known as 'heavenly horses' and were a key part of the Chinese army.

Suddenly, the rhythmic beat of trotting hooves made him turn around. He was confronted by a man leading a fascinating creature of incredible proportions. The horse's body strained with taut muscle as it moved through the crowd, arching its neck and tossing its head. Surely this creation had been sent from heaven — worthy only of gods and emperors.

"These marvellous beasts would be perfect for the Han **cavalry**," Zhang mused to Ganfu. "We must tell the Emperor of this discovery upon our return."

Zhang visited several markets during his travels through the Western Regions.

Journey's End

ELEVEN YEARS AFTER LEAVING CHANG'AN Zhang paced nervously up and down a dusty track. Three moons had passed since he had reached his final destination: the Yuezhi camp.

Upon his arrival, he had been immediately summoned by the Yuezhi leader, King Déshí. Once the introductions had been conducted, they had discussed the proposal. Zhang had been exhausted, thirsty and saddle-sore, but he was determined to strike up an alliance. Much to his frustration, King Déshí had requested some time to consider his options. Since then, Zhang had been terrified that the deal would fall through. What if his mission had been in vain? Had too much time passed? His thoughts were interrupted by a messenger handing him a scroll.

Keen to establish friendly relations with the Han Dynasty, the King of Dayuan provided Zhang with guides and interpreters.

18th May 127 BC

To the esteemed Zhang Qian,

I have carefully considered your offer of an alliance and I write to inform you of my decision.

On the one hand, this is a tempting proposal. We have yet to take revenge for the murder of my father and the barbaric torture inflicted on our people by the Xiongnu. An alliance with the Han Dynasty would therefore provide excellent support if we were to become engaged in battle with these warriors. Furthermore, our respective locations to the east and west flank of the Xiongnu territory would make for a perfect ambush from both sides.

However, this distance is also a reason to reject the union. It would be difficult to form a working alliance at such long range. We have heard much of the difficulties you yourself faced in reaching us. In addition, the lands to which we have been banished by the Xiongnu are actually extremely rich and fertile. We would be reluctant to leave them. The quality of life is good here and we have so far led a peaceful existence, free from invasion. I have no wish to start a war that would threaten this stability.

Taking all of these arguments into account, I have decided to decline your proposition. I hope you understand that this is no reflection on the Han Dynasty or Emperor Wu himself.

Yours sincerely, His Royal Highness, King Déshí of the Yuezhi

The Birth of an Idea

13ᵀᴴ JULY 127 BC Zhang drifted despondently through a market in Bactria (Bac-tree-a). He had long since left the Yuezhi, keen to leave his failure behind him, but he couldn't return to the Emperor empty-handed. He had decided to spend a little time travelling around the Western Regions before going back to Chang'an. Almost nothing was known of the areas to the west of the Han Empire. If Zhang could at least provide the Emperor with some information about these exotic lands, he might escape disgrace. He would distract the Emperor from the failure of the mission by dazzling him with tales of his discoveries.

In the market, he strolled past a stall displaying a collection of goods that seemed familiar to him. There was a piece of bamboo, not unlike the one given to him by Emperor Wu, and a piece of cloth that he knew had come from the Han Empire.

"Good sir," he asked, "how did you come by these items?"

The trader replied, "They are brought here from Qiong (Chee-ong) and Shu in the Han Empire. The merchants travel through Shendu and then on to Bactria. It's a long journey, but it's the only way to avoid the Xiongnu in the north and the barbarian tribes further south. It's worth it though, these items are some of our bestselling goods."

An idea flashed though Zhang's head: how much easier and quicker this trade would be if the goods could travel directly from the Han Empire to Bactria. If only Emperor Wu could gain control of a transport route through the Xiongnu territory, the Han Empire would become an unstoppable commercial force. Perhaps this was the way to appease the Emperor?

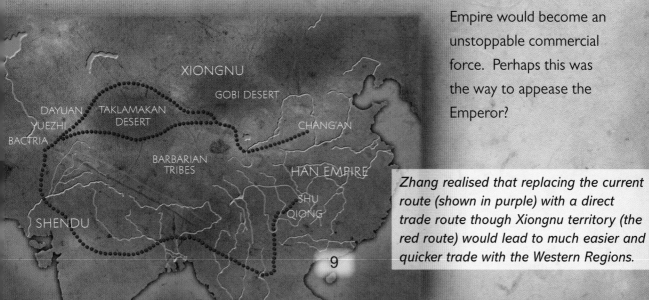

Zhang realised that replacing the current route (shown in purple) with a direct trade route though Xiongnu territory (the red route) would lead to much easier and quicker trade with the Western Regions.

A Rotten State

NOVEMBER 126 BC A fresh wave of nausea broke over Zhang as he bent double to shovel yet more earth into the putrid trench.

Zhang had begun his journey back to the Han Empire a year ago, but his swift progress had been stalled yet again by the Xiongnu. They had captured him, along with Ganfu, his wife and his son, sparing their lives on a whim and returning them to slavery.

Only now, things were ten times worse than the last time he had been enslaved. Zhang was not allowed to see his wife and son, and his new job involved digging **latrines** on the very outer edge of the camp. Every time the tribe moved on, Zhang had to fill in the old trenches and then dig new ones at the next camp. This endless cycle of digging and filling was almost worse than the festering stench. Would he ever see his homeland again? His resilient spirit was nearing its breaking point.

All of a sudden, Ganfu came running up, spluttering and panting with the effort.

"Come quickly!" he shrieked, "There's a fight breaking out in the camp. Now's our chance to escape. The king has died and several of the men are scrabbling for power. The awful brutes and their supporters are fighting each other like idiots. Greed will be the undoing of these barbarian savages."

Zhang and Ganfu charged into the camp, barging their way through the chaos to the tent of a rich aristocrat, where they found Zhang's wife and son cowering in a corner.

There was no time to celebrate their reunion. Grabbing whatever provisions they could find, the small group slipped quietly from the camp, leaving the brawling tribesmen behind.

The Xiongnu were a particularly ferocious tribe of warriors.

© Look and Learn

10

The Hero Returns

OCTOBER 125 BC Zhang lifted his glass and asked everyone in the room to drink a toast to Emperor Wu. The dinner that had been planned in Zhang's honour was in full swing. A jubilant atmosphere filled the room as the assembled men indulged in the delicious food, pausing occasionally to applaud a speech or to salute the returned wanderer.

Zhang brought back several gifts for the Emperor, including an ostrich egg that he had traded for silk in Parthia. The men at court, who had never seen an egg that large, were delighted.

Zhang had received a hero's welcome on his return to Chang'an. Despite being unsuccessful in allying with the Yuezhi, his journey had provided a flood of information on thirty-six different western kingdoms.

The Emperor turned to Zhang: "You have certainly performed a great service to the Empire. You have endured great torment. To think that of more than one hundred men, only you and Ganfu have returned."

"Everything I did, I did for the good of the Dynasty," responded Zhang.

When the time came for the presentation ceremony, Zhang stood and, with a gracious bow, handed the Emperor the bamboo token that he had painstakingly guarded throughout his journey. As the Emperor's fingers closed around the slightly battered stick, Zhang noticed the glimmer of a tear in the corner of his eye. He touched the bamboo token on Zhang's shoulders and announced, "I hereby anoint you Royal Counsellor of the Imperial Palace".

The hall roared with deafening applause that seemed to take forever to subside. Eventually, Zhang and the Emperor were able to resume their seats and the dinner continued.

"You must tell me more about these horses!" whispered the Emperor to his loyal counsellor.

A Chinese silk painting of Emperor Wu outside his palace.

A Remarkable Legacy

DECEMBER 115 BC Zhang relaxed on the terrace. He sat cross-legged on his woven mat and rested one arm on the low table beside him. He inhaled deeply, breathing in the fresh air, and tilted his head back to study the beautiful open skies above Chang'an.

It felt good to be home. He was a natural explorer and usually got itchy feet after spending too long in one place, but something had changed in him. He was an old man now and he had achieved so much — he deserved a rest.

Since his return ten years ago, he had completed another successful journey to the West. He had formed an alliance with the Wusun (Ooh-sen) people and dispatched Han ambassadors across the Western Regions. Now, Han territory was expanding rapidly and trade routes were swiftly developing between China and the West. Zhang felt a sense of personal pride at these developments. Emperor Wu had even appointed him 'Grand Messenger', making him one of the nine most important men in China. Zhang had certainly forged a glittering career as an explorer. He was a pioneer — a born leader who would find eternal fame in the history books of the future.

The Silk Road

The trade route that Zhang Qian established would come to be known as the Silk Road. By 106 BC, it was a regular trade link connecting China to the West.

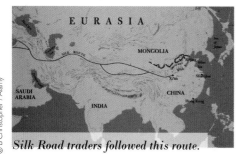

© B Christopher / Alamy

Silk Road traders followed this route.

Where did the Silk Road go?

The Silk Road didn't consist of just one route — it split into several branches. All routes started from the Chinese capital Chang'an, skirted the Great Wall of China and headed up the Gansu Corridor to Dunhuang on the edge of the Taklamakan Desert. At this point, the road split into northern and southern routes.

What was traded along the Silk Road?

The route got its name from Chinese silk, but many other goods were carried from China to the West, including furs, ceramics, jade, bronze ornaments and iron. In turn, China received gold, ivory, glass, exotic animals and plants, precious metals and stones. In addition to introducing these products to a new market, the opening of the Silk Road also resulted in the spread of ideas and religions, most notably Buddhism. The Silk Road carried Buddhist priests and artwork from India to China. Many settlements sprang up along the route, particularly around sources of water, and it was in these towns and cities that most of the trading was done.

What was the journey like?

Travellers were constantly threatened by a lack of water and the risk of disease (the **Black Death** was reportedly spread along the Silk Road in the 1340s, killing millions of people). Attacks from bandits were also common. However, this did little to deter the huge numbers of traders, merchants and adventurers. The most famous traveller of the Silk Road was Marco Polo, a European explorer who wrote extensive accounts of the Chinese Empire.

The development of the Silk Road continued throughout the Middle Ages.

© North Wind Picture Archives / Alamy

Glossary

alliance — A promise of assistance and protection between two nations

ambassador — A representative of one country who is sent to another country

aristocrat — A person who belongs to the upper class

Black Death — A plague that spread from Asia to Europe, killing millions of people

cavalry — Troops mounted on horseback

dignitary — A high-ranking official

latrines — Holes dug in the ground to be used as toilets

pioneers — People who explore new territories

porters — People who are employed to carry luggage and supplies

David Livingstone

"Fighting to free Africa from slavery"

written by Claire Boulter

FEBRUARY 1844, MABOTSA, SOUTH AFRICA Crouched on the hill, the lion prepares to pounce. David takes a step towards the beast, takes aim. He fires — once, twice.

The lion is wounded, but still full of life. In slow motion it springs at him. He feels the warmth of its breath on his cheek. He sees its gaping jaws descend. He hears his bones snap like dry twigs. Oddly, he feels no fear, no pain. Not yet.

He is surprised to find himself on the ground. The world starts to go dark. He can just make out his friend Mebalwe (Meb-al-we), desperately loading his rifle. The lion has seen him too; the weight on David's body lifts as the creature whirls and leaps at Mebalwe, seizing his leg.

Another man stabs at the lion with a spear. It grabs him by the shoulder, tries to shake him, but its movements are heavy now. It staggers, falls.

His eyes now closed, his body numb, David can only hear. As darkness floods his mind he offers a simple prayer — perhaps his last — to the God who led him to Africa.

Anxious villagers crowd around his still body, hoping for a sign of life. His chest rises slightly and a shout goes up.

"He's alive!"

This sculpture of David being attacked by the lion was created by Gareth Knowles.

Labour and Learning

SEPTEMBER 1824, BLANTYRE, SCOTLAND Propping up a Latin book on the **spinning machine** in front of him, eleven-year-old David bit his lip and tried to block out the roar and clatter of machinery. The air in the mill was hot and thick with cotton dust, and David had to squint to read the page in front of him. Frowning slightly, his lips formed the shape of the unfamiliar words.

In the early 19th century, it was common for children from poor families to work. Many children worked twelve hour days in dirty, dangerous conditions.

A sudden lull in the shouts and laughter of the other boys alerted him to the arrival of their supervisor. With a sigh, David turned from his book to check on the threads of cotton spinning on the huge wheels. His job was to mend these threads whenever it looked like they were about to break. He had been doing this for a year now: up at 5.30, in the mill for 6, then twelve hours of work, followed by two hours of lessons. It was hard, dull work, but his family needed his wages.

David smiled as he remembered that tomorrow was Sunday, a rest day. After church, he decided, he would continue his exploration of the moors behind his house. His habit, as he roamed, was to dream of the bright, unwritten future and all the wonderful places that he had read about. He knew that one day he would do more than dream.

"...books of travels were my especial delight"

© iStockphoto.com/jgshields

David, his parents and his four siblings lived in a single room in this building. The building is now a museum dedicated to his life.

The Man and the Mission

MAY 1834, BLANTYRE Seated in a sheltered hollow on the hillside above the village, David frowned intently at the booklet in his hands. It was an appeal for medical **missionaries** to travel to remote, mysterious areas of the world. For years now he had wanted more from life than Blantyre could offer. He had done well at school and had been promoted at the mill, but to spend the rest of his life there... the thought was unbearable!

A smile spread across David's face as his future came into sharp focus. As a missionary, he would be able to help people who had even less than he did. Closing the booklet, he vowed to save every penny, study medicine and religion, then go wherever he was needed most.

MISSION OR MISTAKE?

When missionaries like David Livingstone set out for far-flung countries, they were not only trying to spread Christianity, but also to help the people they met. While they did have some positive impacts, they also caused problems for the people they tried to assist.

Many countries had little knowledge of or access to up-to-date medicine. Missionaries were able to treat illnesses and injuries that had previously been incurable. Sadly, they also unknowingly carried diseases, such as measles and smallpox, which killed many people.

Missionaries often set up schools to educate the local people, teaching them not only how to read and write but also how to farm their land efficiently. However, many missionaries thought their own culture, religion and language were better than those of the locals, and did not teach them about local history, beliefs or traditions.

A mission school in Africa

By introducing European clothing, food and utensils, missionaries increased the range of goods available. On the other hand, the natives had previously produced everything that they needed. If they wanted the new goods they had to buy them, which meant that they had to change their whole way of life to start making money.

Overall, missionaries had much to offer the countries that they travelled to, such as better healthcare, education and access to products from around the world. However, by enforcing European views and beliefs on the local people, the missionaries suppressed their culture and changed the way they lived forever.

The Smoke of a Thousand Villages

MAY 1841, SOUTH AFRICA Trudging along the dusty track beside the ox-drawn wagon, David smiled. After the tedious, backbreaking years in the cotton mill and the late nights poring over medical books, the open horizons of Africa spelt freedom.

Two months had passed since he landed in Cape Town and set off for Kuruman — the most inland **mission station** in South Africa. He had grown used to the spiced honey smell of the spiny acacia trees, the distant howls and roars of unseen animals, the antelope that froze for a second, quivering, then bounded gracefully away. It was a far cry from Scotland.

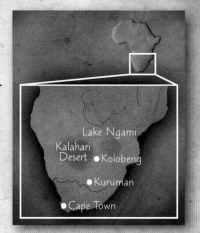

OCTOBER 1841, KURUMAN Standing outside the mission buildings, David watched the African sun rise slowly over the distant hills. In the hut behind him he heard the other missionaries starting to stir, and he gave a deep sigh.

He had been at Kuruman for several months now. At first it had seemed like everything he had hoped for. The local people were friendly, willing to learn about Christianity and grateful for David's medical skills. However, as time wore on he began to feel useless. There were so many missionaries here — far more than the small village needed — yet further into Africa there were none. The words of another missionary rang in David's ears.

"In the vast plain to the north I have sometimes seen... the smoke of a thousand villages where no missionary has ever been"

David squinted to the north. Suddenly, a smile lit his face. He wasn't needed here; he would go north, in search of the distant smoke.

The mission station at Kuruman included this church, a school, and houses for the missionaries.

The Thirsty Earth

NOVEMBER 1847, KOLOBENG David stretched and stood back to survey the latest **irrigation** ditch that he and the native men had dug. A ragged cheer went up from the men around him as the river water started to seep into the ditch and trickle towards their crops and gardens. The Bakwena (Bak-wain-a) tribe had initially been reluctant to try David's idea — they had their own rain doctor to summon the rains — and he knew it was a sign of how much they had come to trust and respect him that they had eventually agreed to it.

Later that evening, David sat quietly in his hut watching his wife nurse their baby daughter. As his tired body slipped towards sleep, David's mind drifted. So much had happened since he left Kuruman — he had seen so many sights, met so many people, got married, had children. He had even survived a lion attack! Now, at last, he had found a place where he could make a difference, a place where he belonged.

A YEAR LATER David sat in a circle with the tribal elders, glaring up at the cloudless sky.

"The rains have failed." Sechéle (Say-shell-ay), the Bakwena chief, sounded tired. "The river is dry. The crops are dying. Our wives and children are suffering. We must leave here."

David sighed and shook his head sorrowfully. The work he had started here would remain undone; the people would have to move elsewhere. As for him, he would have to leave the first real home he had known in years.

David's brow knitted as a memory struggled to the surface of his mind. He remembered hearing of a great lake, somewhere north of here, in a rich, fertile land that was home to great numbers of people. The lake shimmered at the edge of David's imagination, drawing him northward again.

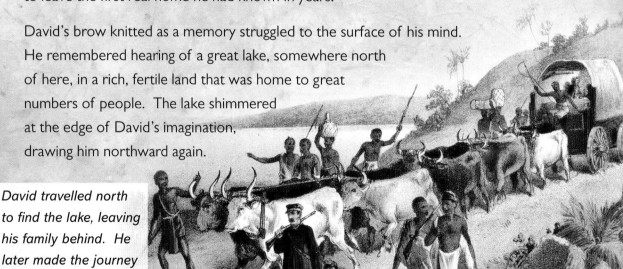

David travelled north to find the lake, leaving his family behind. He later made the journey with his family.

© Photos.com/Thinkstock.com

JULY 1849, KALAHARI DESERT Pausing for a moment to rest, David shook his water bottle and raised it to his mouth. A single drop of liquid fell onto his parched tongue. He tried to swallow, but his mouth was as dry as the sand beneath his boots.

"Come," the voice of his guide Ramotobi (Ram-oh-toby) came as if from a great distance, "we must carry on. Water is nearby, but if we stop now we will never reach it."

The name 'Kalahari' comes from the word 'Kgala'. In Tswana, an African language, 'Kgala' means 'the great thirst'.

They had been travelling for over a month now, surviving off the meagre water supplies that Ramotobi was able to find. If they didn't find more water soon, David knew that he would die in this remote, sun-scorched corner of the globe. With a mighty effort, he placed one foot in front of the other and staggered onwards.

They had been walking for several more hours when David was shaken from his plodding stupor by a shout from ahead. Looking up, he saw a thin green line on the horizon — trees! David stood still as stone, gazing ahead, drinking in the promise of water.

How to Find Water in the Desert

Humans can't survive in the desert for more than a few days without water. If you're planning a trip, follow these tips to help you find water in the most barren of places.

1. Scout out dry river channels. Sometimes water still flows beneath the surface. When you find one, dig. If there's water there it will fill the hole.

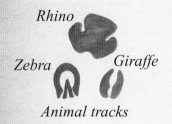

Rhino
Zebra *Giraffe*
Animal tracks

2. Look for wildlife. Animals such as rhinos, giraffes and zebras can't survive for long without water, so if you spot them water can't be more than 7 or 8 miles distant. Make sure you can recognise the tracks of these creatures, so that you can follow them towards water.

3. Learn to identify native vegetation. Certain plants grow a tuber (a large root) to store water, which can be dug up and eaten. To the right is a plant known locally as Leroshua. 12 to 18 inches below the plant is a tuber, often as large as a child's head. The water it contains is fresh and cold.

4. Watch for smoke and lines of trees. Trees often mark the course of a river, while smoke shows that people, and therefore water, are near.

Leroshua

A Land in Chains

AUGUST 1851, NORTH OF LAKE NGAMI (UN-GARM-EE) David lifted his young son gently on to the wagon, biting his lip as he felt the boy's burning skin. The area had seemed so promising as a place to settle that David had journeyed back to Kolobeng to bring his family north. But the lake and river valleys had turned out to be treacherous, unhealthy places. His children were ill with fever, and with his wife pregnant again it was clear that she and the children couldn't stay here. David knew that the safest place for them was England.

He was torn — it would break his heart to part with them, but he couldn't give up on Africa, not now. For he had a new dream — ten days ago, he had discovered a broad river, which he suspected flowed all the way to the coast. If he was right, traders and missionaries would be able to travel into the centre of Africa with the greatest of ease!

SEPTEMBER 1852, KOLOBENG Replaying his last glimpse of the children's small faces as they waved goodbye from the ship in Cape Town harbour, David initially saw nothing wrong with his home in Kolobeng as he approached. It was only as he drew closer that he noticed something was amiss. Where were the animals that should be grazing in the pasture? Where were the people who should be tending the crops?

A cold dread gripped David as he pushed open the door to his house — why wasn't it locked? Inside, all was chaos. The furniture was smashed, his books torn and burnt, his medicine bottles shattered. David tensed as he heard a small sound outside, then relaxed as a small girl stepped timidly into the room.

"They're all gone!" she sobbed. "The bad men came. My parents are dead, my brothers taken. Our friends and neighbours too — all dead or stolen."

David clenched his fists. He knew who had done this: the slave traders, who bought and sold humans as though they were objects. He must stop them. In that instant, he made a vow to himself:

"I shall open up a path to the interior or perish"

Men, women and children were taken as slaves.

Journal Entry, 20th September 1852
How can the slave trade be stopped?

The slave trade has been going on for centuries, and millions of African people have been enslaved. The transport of slaves across the Atlantic is now illegal, and many of us do what we can to fight it on land, while anti-slave ships patrol the ocean. However, many traders continue to break the law. The vile practice of enslaving men, women and children must stop, and I believe that the answer lies in opening a route from the coast to the centre of Africa.

How are African people enslaved?

Many Africans are captured by slave traders, who raid villages and seize as many people as they can. In addition, in wars between different tribes, prisoners are often taken by the winning side. The tribes are so keen to acquire European goods such as guns, ploughs, spades and soap that they are prepared to exchange their prisoners for such items.

Once enslaved, African men, women and children are commonly marched to the coast. From there, they are transported to America and the Caribbean, where they work on plantations and in mines.

How would a route into the centre of Africa help?

An easy route into the centre of Africa would allow honest traders to supply African tribes with the goods that they desire, in exchange for local products such as ivory, ostrich feathers and beeswax. By providing the tribes with an alternative means of obtaining European goods, the swapping of prisoners for goods would cease.

A safe route to the more remote parts of Africa would make it easier to get there, which would encourage more traders and missionaries to settle there. Many European countries are trying to enforce the ban on the Atlantic slave trade, so slave traders avoid Europeans for fear of punishment. It therefore stands to reason that a greater concentration of European people in Africa will help to end the slave trade once and for all.

A trade route could stretch from the interior to the east or west coast.

Coast to Coast

NOVEMBER 1853, LINYANTI David checked through the supplies one more time as the small group of men who would accompany him loaded them into the canoe. He would take only what he needed to survive, plus his Bible and his journal. For everything else, he would have to rely on the bounty of the land and the generosity of the people he met.

As he pushed his canoe off from the grassy bank and paddled upstream, David felt his spirit soar. Green and yellow parrots squawked in the trees; hippopotami surfaced to regard the passers-by with curious eyes; acid-green iguanas basked on low-hanging branches. This was the start of an adventure!

While travelling, David came up with a recipe for tablets to treat malaria — a serious disease spread by mosquitoes. Sold as 'Livingstone's Rousers', they saved many lives.

FEBRUARY 1854, THE UPPER ZAMBEZI Wiping the rain from his eyes with his sopping sleeve, David swung his axe at the dense mass of trees and vines. The world was a damp, dull green, the midday light muted by the impenetrable thicket that surrounded them.

Miles of roaring rapids had made the river route impassable, and they had been forced to abandon the canoes and continue on foot. Despite the warmth of the day, David shivered — the close, mosquito-clogged air of the river had left him with a fever that made his head spin and his legs feel weak. Every step was a challenge, but there was no alternative. He must go on.

MAY 1854, LUANDA David stood on a rise above the town, barely seeing the fine buildings that sunned themselves beside the glittering sea. They had made it to the coast, but the achievement gave him no pleasure. The journey had been plagued by dense jungle, reeking marshes, treacherous rapids, hungry crocodiles, disease-ridden insects... there was no safe route from the interior to the west coast. There was nothing for it but to retrace his steps.

© Classic Image / Alamy

Luanda in the 19th century.

SEPTEMBER 1855, LINYANTI Sekeletu (Sek-ell-et-oo), chief of the Makololo tribe, called a greeting as a straggling group of men limped into the village. It took him a moment to recognise the thin, ill-looking white man who slumped onto a wooden bench.

"My friend, is it really you?" he asked, his voice full of concern.

A ring of people gathered round as David, with many pauses, recounted the journey from Luanda — the fevers they had all suffered from, the lack of food, the run-ins with unfriendly tribes and slave traders.

"So now you'll stay here with us." Sekeletu's words were a statement, not a question.

"No, no," David replied at once. "I'll rest a little, that's all. The country to the west isn't suitable, but as soon as I'm strong again I'll travel east. I *will* find a good path to the coast."

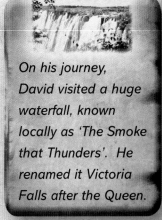

MAY 1856, QUELIMANE (KEL-IM-ARN-EE) Sailing down the river in a borrowed boat, David leaned against the railing and gazed to the future. In his mind's eye, he saw trading ships skimming past each other, laden with valuable produce. With the exception of one set of rapids, the river could be navigated by large boats for six hundred miles. What's more, the country he had passed through was rich and fertile — crops flourished and iron, gold and coal were abundant. David knew that if he could persuade European traders that this was a good trade route, they could supply the natives with everything that they wanted. The slave trade would be dealt a fatal blow!

On his journey, David visited a huge waterfall, known locally as 'The Smoke that Thunders'. He renamed it Victoria Falls after the Queen.

All that remained was to convince the traders that they should give Africa a chance. For that, he would have to return to England.

Between 1854 and 1856, David travelled right across Africa.

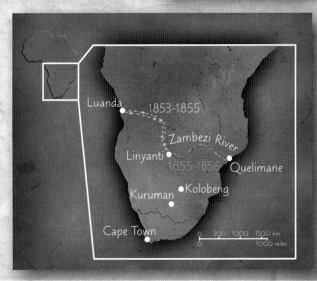

23

A Stranger in a Strange Land

JANUARY 1857, LONDON Walking up the steps to the stage, David looked out across the sea of expectant faces. He had already given several talks, but the number of people who came to hear him speak still surprised him. Although he had felt cut off from events in Britain while he had been away, his travels had been written about in newspapers and magazines. Everywhere he went, he was greeted as a hero. Merely walking down the street was strange enough, but to be recognised and greeted by everyone he saw was truly bizarre.

As he started to describe the horrors of the slave trade, he prayed that his words would make a difference. If only the merchants and missionaries would listen to him and travel to Africa.

David with his wife and children in Britain in 1858.

© Pictorial Press Ltd / Alamy

Letters to the editor   London, 16th January 1857

Dear Sir,

We must act now to help our African brothers and to stop the cruel and barbaric practice of slavery.

If you saw a young boy beaten in the street, would you not step in to protect him? If you saw a woman stumble for lack of food and rest, and be whipped for stumbling, would you not help her?

Last night I heard Dr. David Livingstone speak. His tales of the brutal treatment of our African brothers and sisters filled me with disgust, horror and shame. Disgust that children as young as three are stolen from their families and sold like animals. Horror that across the world millions of people live in fear and pain. Shame that, for so long, I have closed my eyes to this suffering.

Our path is clear — we must follow where Dr. Livingstone leads. Africa needs missionaries to spread the word of God. *Let us be missionaries*. Africa needs businessmen to teach her how to rise from poverty to greatness. *Let us be businessmen*. Let each of us do our duty to this poor, plagued continent. Let us free Africa from violence and injustice.

Yours faithfully,
James Tremayne, Esq.

Rumour and Relief

DECEMBER 1866, ZANZIBAR The British officials' eyes turned anxiously to the door as Musa, one of David's guides, shuffled into the room, his head bowed. Eight years had passed since David had returned to Africa to continue his plans for a trade route, but nobody had heard from him for some time. Still staring at the floor, Musa began to speak.

"Sirs, I am here to tell you that Dr. Livingstone is dead. He was set on by wicked, violent men. He tried to fight them, but there were too many. I fled, in fear for my life, and when I returned I found his body. I buried him in the jungle close to Lake Nyassa (Nee-assa)."

OCTOBER 1871, UJIJI (OO-JEE-JEE) Henry Stanley emerged from the green silence of the jungle into a large clearing, full of noise and life. Women sat grinding corn, laughing quietly together, and small children shrieked as they chased each other around the huts. The children fell silent as they saw Henry. After a moment, a thin, slightly stooped figure emerged from a shady doorway. Henry grinned broadly and strode forward.

Musa lied about David's death because he knew that he wouldn't get paid if he admitted that he had abandoned David.

"Dr. Livingstone, I presume?"

The sun sank below the horizon and the silver moon rose as Henry filled David in on everything that was happening outside of Africa, including the rumours of David's death.

"Not everyone believed that you were dead," explained Henry, "so I came to track you down. I can't begin to tell you how glad I am to find you alive. But look here: you've done all you can to open up Africa to commerce and stop the accursed slave trade. It's clear that you're not in good health — isn't it time that you came home?"

David sighed. "Sometimes I'd like nothing more, but I cannot leave until my work is done."

© Look and Learn

Henry Stanley was a journalist who had been sent to find David.

The Final Journey

29TH APRIL 1873, CHITAMBO (CHIT-AM-BO) David groaned as his friends, Susi and Chuma, lifted him gently from the **kitanda** to the bed of dried grass. Through his fever David was vaguely aware of Susi moving around the hut, occasionally straightening his blanket or holding a cup of water to his parched lips.

The hours blurred together, until David finally surfaced from a dream of rain on Scottish moors, his head clear for the first time in days. The hut was dark and still. Wincing, he shifted his legs gingerly to the ground. Kneeling by the bed, he bent his head in prayer.

Some hours later, Susi crept quietly into the hut. He touched David's shoulder gently, then jerked his hand back. The body was cold; David's spirit had fled.

As dawn spread soft, silver wings over the remote African village, Susi and Chuma made whispered plans. David's body must be returned to England so his family could say goodbye. They would carry him the thousand miles or more, through jungle and swamp, across river and mountain, to the coast, where a ship would bear his body across the ocean. First though, they both agreed, his heart must be buried under a tree in the village.

A month after David's death, African leaders agreed to stop the slave trade on the east coast. In time, the route David found from Quelimane to Lake Nyassa brought trade and commerce to Africa.

"You can have his body, but his heart belongs in Africa!"

Glossary

irrigation — Applying water to the land to help crops grow

kitanda — A stretcher that is hung from a pole so it can be carried

mission station — A place set up by missionaries, from which they work

missionaries — Members of a religious group who travel to an area to convert the people there to their religion

spinning machine — A machine which spins cotton fibre into thread

Nellie Bly

"The World's favourite reporter"

written by Paul Jordin

17ᵀᴴ JANUARY 1885 "Mother, just look at this column in *The Dispatch*!" fumed Elizabeth, as she slammed the newspaper down on the table. "I've never read such poppycock! Who does this Erasmus Wilson think he is? Look, he says women shouldn't have a job, or even an education!"

Looking at the paper, her mother tutted. "You're quite right. This fellow clearly needs setting straight on a few things."

"My thoughts exactly," Elizabeth replied, with a steely glint in her eye, "and I'm going to do the setting!"

Elizabeth Cochrane (Coc-ran), later known as Nellie Bly, was born on the 5ᵗʰ May 1864 in Pennsylvania, USA.

Burning with anger, she stomped to her room to pen a fiery response to the article. Why shouldn't she work if she wanted to? She had as much right as any man! And what about women like her own mother? She'd been married three times, but after being widowed twice, then divorcing her third husband, she was determined to provide for her family herself. In Elizabeth's opinion, that was a reason to be proud, not ashamed!

A FEW DAYS LATER Elizabeth smiled politely as she was introduced to George Madden, editor of *The Pittsburgh Dispatch*. After reading her letter, he'd invited her to visit the newspaper offices. She'd been surprised to find that the staff weren't the cross old men she'd expected. Even Erasmus Wilson was courteous and good-natured in person.

Mr Madden looked again at her letter on the desk in front of him. "I read your letter, Miss Cochrane," he said. "Your grammar and punctuation leave a lot to be desired... but I like your style. I like your spirit. How would you like to write a piece for my paper?"

The city of Pittsburgh, where the young Nellie Bly lived.

"Nellie Bly, Reporter"

25TH JANUARY 1885 Elizabeth's eyes shone with pride as she looked at the day's paper. Her own words, in print! She could hardly believe it. What's more, Mr Madden liked her article so much he had offered her a full-time job writing for *The Dispatch*.

She couldn't wait to get started! She had plans for a series of articles about the women who worked in Pittsburgh's factories. She would show the Erasmus Wilsons of this world what life for poor women in the city was really like.

Mr Madden had insisted that as a professional reporter she would need a pen name. In the end he had picked 'Nellie Bly'. Now Elizabeth stood in front of the mirror, looking herself in the eye. She offered her hand to her reflection. "Nellie Bly, reporter. Pleased to meet you."

Female journalists in Nellie Bly's day often used pen names. The name 'Nellie Bly' was inspired by the title of a popular song.

The Pittsburgh Dispatch

PITTSBURGH, TUESDAY, FEBRUARY 17, 1885 — 3¢

WHERE ARE THE ERRAND GIRLS? BY NELLIE BLY

It is both foolish and unfair that young girls do not have the same opportunities as boys when they start out in the world of work.

For example, there is no good reason why the job of errand 'boy' couldn't be done by a girl. A young man may start as an errand boy and work his way up through the firm. Girls are just as smart, just as keen, just as quick to learn, so why can't they do the same?

Instead, we banish even the smartest, keenest, quickest young women to dark, dismal, dangerous factories. There is little chance in a factory for a girl to expand her mind, to progress within the company, or even to earn a decent wage. What a waste of her talent, her youth, her energy!

Many wealthy, great and powerful men came from humble beginnings; this country was built by such men. If only we gave young women the same chances, wouldn't we have twice as many great people? Wouldn't America grow to be twice as great, and do so twice as fast?

Thousands of girls in this city have no choice but to work. If you own a business, big or small, you can do better for them. You *must* do better for them. And you can start today, simply by hiring an errand girl.

Flowers and Frustration

JUNE 1885 Nellie's first few months of reporting had gone well. She had written about the struggles of working women and life in Pittsburgh's factories, all the time learning as much as she could from her fellow reporters. Now, she fidgeted slightly as she sat opposite Mr Madden, eager to hear what new assignment he had in store for her.

"Now, Nellie," he began, "I've got a bit of a change planned for you. I need someone to write for the women's pages. Obviously, as a woman, you're well qualified for that. First off, the Summer Flower Show opens tomorrow..."

Nellie sagged with disappointment. Flower show? That wasn't news! Still, she had a job to do. If Nellie Bly was going to write a report about a flower show, it would be the best darn flower show report Pittsburgh had ever seen!

The 'women's pages' covered topics like fashion, cookery and gossip about the rich and famous. In Nellie's day, many people thought these were the only things women should be interested in.

MAY 1887 It was late in the evening and most of the paper's staff had gone home for the day. Nellie broke the silence of the office with a loud sigh as she tossed her pen aside.

She read through what she had just written: an empty bit of fluff about summer hats. No wonder the male journalists at *The Dispatch* thought writing for the women's pages was beneath them. It dawned on Nellie that as long as she stayed here, she would be trapped in a frilly, silly, pastel-tinted, sugar-coated, floral-scented prison.

Her hand trembling slightly, Nellie grabbed a scrap of paper and scribbled a short note. She looked around, wondering where best to leave it. Her eyes fell on Erasmus Wilson's desk. Perfect! After all, without him she might never have become a journalist. She placed the note next to his coffee cup. Then she gathered her things, took a deep breath and walked out of the offices of *The Pittsburgh Dispatch*.

The next morning, Erasmus Wilson walked into George Madden's office and handed him the note without a word. It said simply:

"I'm off for New York. Look out for me. Bly."

In at the Deep End

AUGUST 1887 Nellie bit her lip as John Cockerill, editor of *The New York World*, studied the story ideas she had brought in. Most of the editors in New York thought a newsroom was no place for a woman, but after weeks of rejections, she had finally got a job interview.

"Well sir," she said finally, "if you don't wish to hire me, this isn't the only paper in New York…" She hoped her voice didn't betray just how desperately she wanted the job.

"No need for that, Miss Bly. I'm going to give you a shot," Cockerill replied. "I've got a story in mind that an unknown reporter like you could be perfect for — if you're up to the challenge."

Nellie listened, excitement mingling with fear as he explained what he wanted her to do. It would be a difficult, frightening, even dangerous assignment. It would also be a chance to make a name for herself, and she was determined to grab it with both hands.

Park Row, home of New York's newspaper offices in the 1880s.

25ᵀᴴ SEPTEMBER 1887 Dr Matthew Field regarded the patient in front of him, a young woman named Nellie Brown. Miss Brown had moved into a boarding house two days earlier. She had frightened the other residents by acting strangely and talking nonsense, so a court had declared her insane and sent her here, to Bellevue Hospital.

The doctor asked Miss Brown a few questions. The poor creature didn't seem to understand half of them. Today she thought her name might be Mareno, not Brown, and that maybe she came from Cuba, but that was all she could remember. Dr Field sighed — another hopeless case.

The next day, Nellie Brown was transferred to the **notorious** Blackwell's Island **Asylum**. Unlike the other women who were sent there, being taken to Blackwell's Island was exactly what she wanted. For Nellie Brown was in fact Nellie Bly, working undercover to investigate the asylum.

WHO IS THIS INSANE GIRL?
SHE IS PRETTY, WELL DRESSED AND SPEAKS SPANISH.

STILL A MYSTERY.
NELLIE MARENO'S FRIENDS AS SILENT AS SHE WAS HERSELF

HER MEMORY STILL GONE
NO ONE CLAIMS THE PRETTY CRAZY GIRL AT BELLEVUE

Nellie even fooled her fellow journalists. While she was in the hospital, several papers printed stories about the 'mysterious insane girl' who'd lost her memory.

3ʳᵈ OCTOBER 1887 Nellie shifted on the hard bench, where the women were forced to sit in silence for hours on end, day after day. Her stomach groaned with hunger, but she dreaded facing another meal of foul-smelling, greenish meat and stale, jaw-breaking bread. Her head ached with tiredness, but she knew the cries and screams of the other women would keep her awake again tonight. Life inside the asylum was even worse than Nellie had expected. Most of the nurses were cruel bullies, while the doctors didn't seem to do anything at all.

A bone-chilling draught gusted through the foul, grimy room. Nellie flinched as a rat scurried across the dirty floor. Beside her, her new friend Tillie rocked gently back and forth, shivering. Tillie had arrived suffering from stress and depression, not insanity. She had arrived thinking she would get help. Instead, her mental state was worsening by the day.

In a couple of days, a lawyer from *The New York World* would be coming to have Nellie released. She clung to that comforting thought, and tried not to think about how she might cope without it.

Asylums: What Went Wrong?

Lunatic asylums were built to provide a calm, safe environment where people with mental illnesses could be looked after. However, many became fearsome places that did more harm than good. The main reason for this was overcrowding.

Inside the Blackwell's Island Asylum

The overcrowding happened because there were no clear rules about who should be sent to the asylums. They therefore became dumping grounds for the homeless, elderly and disabled, as well as those with genuine mental illnesses.

There was not enough money to care for the large numbers of patients, so asylums often couldn't provide decent food for them or heat the buildings adequately during winter. Many asylums couldn't even afford to hire enough doctors and nurses. As a consequence, the staff they did employ were always overstretched. This meant that it was very hard for them to help anyone get better. Patients ended up staying in the asylums for longer, so the overcrowding became even worse.

As asylums filled up, strained budgets meant that conditions inside worsened, which in turn meant that patients got worse, not better. In this way, the entire system became trapped in a vicious circle of overcrowding and underfunding.

Making a Difference

THREE WEEKS LATER Nellie suppressed a shiver as she passed through the front door of the asylum. She hadn't expected to be back on Blackwell's Island so soon. Her reports about the asylum had caused a sensation. The government had launched an investigation and Nellie had been asked to assist the investigators.

Today, they had come to see the asylum for themselves. Nellie could hardly believe this was the same building in which she had been locked up. It was as if the whole place had been reflected in a magic mirror: floors that had been filthy now sparkled; stale bread had been replaced by soft, fresh loaves; once-shivering shoulders were now snug in warm blankets; even the unfriendly scowls on the nurses' faces had become kindly smiles.

The investigators agreed with all the changes Nellie recommended. They arranged extra funding to improve all the asylums in New York.

Nellie helped the investigators to interview the patients — many of them remembered her, and it calmed them to see a familiar face. One woman remarked how odd it was that things had started improving just after 'Miss Brown' left. Little did she know how much she had to thank Nellie for!

OCTOBER 1888 Nellie drummed her fingers on her desk as she gazed at the moonlit street below her window. Sometimes, new ideas for stories came easily. Tonight, all she had produced was an overflowing waste paper basket and a well-chewed pencil.

In the year since her asylum **scoop**, she had gone from strength to strength, attacking each new assignment with relish. One week she might go undercover to expose corrupt politicians or phony doctors. The next she could be trying her hand at being a ballet dancer, or training with a ladies' fencing team. Whatever the story, Nellie was the star, and the public loved reading about her latest adventures.

Nellie's popularity had made the editors of New York's papers sit up and take notice. Suddenly, there were lots of 'girl reporters' at work in the city. *The World* had three of its own, including Nellie. If she wanted to stay at the top, Nellie needed a new story. She dreamt of writing something that would still be talked about years, even decades, from now. But what...?

A Great Adventure

NOVEMBER 1888 Nellie swept into her editor's office and dropped a book on his desk.

"*Around the World in Eighty Days*," she said. "I want to do it for real. Not just match the story, but beat it. I've done some research, it should be possible in seventy-five if..."

Mr Cockerill interrupted her with a chuckle and a shake of his head. "Well, it's a good idea, I'll give you that — but it's not a job for a woman. You couldn't possibly travel alone, without a protector! Not to mention all the luggage a lady traveller would need... No-one but a man could do this."

'Around the World in Eighty Days' was written by the French author Jules Verne. It tells the story of Phileas Fogg, who must get around the globe in eighty days to win a bet.

"Very well," snapped Nellie, "start the man, and I'll start the same day for some other newspaper and beat him."

He looked at her for a few moments. "Yes, I believe you would," he replied. "Leave it with me. I'll consider it."

14TH NOVEMBER 1889 Nellie gazed back from the deck of the *Augusta Victoria*. Behind her, New York was just a jumble of matchboxes. She tried to convince herself that she could still see her friends and family waving on the quayside, though they were long out of sight. The only figure she could still make out was Lady Liberty; the statue's arm was raised as if to say, "Goodbye Nellie Bly! Goodbye and good luck!"

It was almost exactly a year since she had taken her round-the-world idea to Mr Cockerill. She thought he had forgotten about it; she had almost forgotten it herself. Then, out of the blue, he summoned her to his office and asked simply, "Can you start around the world the day after tomorrow?"

Of course, she said yes.

Nellie breathed in a great lungful of briny air, then turned away from New York with a lump in her throat and a whole swarm of butterflies in her stomach. No going back now — she was on her way!

Nellie Bly in her travelling outfit.

A Meeting of Minds

DAY 8 — AMIENS (AM-YAN), FRANCE Nellie told herself it was silly to be nervous. She had met famous people before. Why, she was famous herself! Still, she wished she could wash her face and tidy up her hair. She did so want to make a good impression.

She stepped down from the train, her heart pounding. Waiting to greet her on the platform was the snowy-haired gentleman she had travelled out of her way to visit: Monsieur (Mus-yur) Jules Verne, one of the most famous authors in the world, and the man whose writing had inspired her own voyage.

She could scarcely believe it. Little Elizabeth Cochrane, shaking Jules Verne's hand, meeting Jules Verne's charming wife! Going to visit Jules Verne's home, sipping a glass of Jules Verne's wine and being shown around Jules Verne's study!

She stayed as long as she dared, savouring every moment, until it was time to rush back to the station. She made the train with just moments to spare. As it pulled away, Nellie sank back in her seat with a contented sigh. She wouldn't have missed that for anything!

DAY 24 — COLOMBO, CEYLON (SELL-ON) Nellie laughed as the spray flicked up into her face. Back on the ship, the other passengers were still jostling to get onto the little steamboats that had gathered to carry them ashore. Meanwhile, Nellie had hopped aboard a tiny **catamaran**, which now skimmed cheekily across the harbour.

The stifling heat while they had been at sea had made the past two weeks stretch out like an eternity. Like a child waiting for Christmas, Nellie had willed Ceylon (modern-day Sri Lanka) to appear on the horizon. What a relief to finally see its trees and green hills, to feel a fresh, cooling breeze on her cheek!

Although the journey here had felt slow, at least she had been moving. Nellie's next ship wasn't due to leave Ceylon for five days. She planned to take a train to the mountains, visit ancient temples, go to the theatre; anything to distract herself from the agonising wait. But all the while, she knew the clock would be ticking...

© Mary Evans Picture Library

Traditional catamarans.

34

An Unwelcome Surprise

DAY 39 — HONG KONG It was two days until Christmas, but as she slumped onto her hotel bed, Nellie felt far from festive and very far from home. She was determined not to let anyone here see her true feelings about the day's events, but she didn't want to bottle them up either. She fished in her bag for a pen and paper. A letter to her sister wasn't as good as a conversation, but it would have to do.

Monday, December 23rd 1889, Hong Kong

Dear Catherine,

I've just had an awful surprise! I arrived in Hong Kong this morning, two days ahead of time, so I felt pretty pleased with myself. Then I went to book my ticket to Japan — and found out something that ruined my good mood.

The man in the ticket office told me that another girl reporter is travelling around the world in the opposite direction. Apparently, this copycat even set off the same day I did! He seemed very pleased with himself when he realised I didn't know. I suppose I'm the last person in the whole world to find out! I can't believe Cockerill hasn't sent a telegram to tell me about this!

Even worse, the man cheerfully told me that the other girl passed this way three days ago and that I am on course to be beaten. Of course, I tried to remain calm — I didn't want the man to see he'd rattled me — but inside I felt sick. I insisted I'm only racing the clock, though perhaps I insisted too hard. The look in the man's eye told me he didn't believe that for a second.

Still, there's nothing I can do about this other girl. Apparently she thinks she can do the trip in 70 days. Well, good luck to her! I promised to get home in 75 days, and if I can do that, I'll be satisfied. Oh, but I do so want to get home first!

You won't get this till next year, but I'll wish you Merry Christmas anyway: Merry Christmas and Happy New Year!

With love, your sister Elizabeth

Nellie's rival was Elizabeth Bisland, a magazine journalist. When her editor heard about Nellie's trip, he sent Elizabeth to try to beat her.

Nellie spent Christmas Day 1889 in Canton, China.

© World History Archive / Alamy

An Ocean of Trouble

DAY 55 — PACIFIC OCEAN *The Oriental* pitched and rolled on the stormy sea. All around the ship, the waves were grey-green sea serpents, writhing and thrashing. Nellie sat by a window, unable to tear herself away from the scene. As a flash of lightning lit her worried face, she imagined precious hours and miles slipping away beneath the waves. The storm outside continued to howl, and Nellie wanted to howl with it.

She tried to comfort herself by thinking back to what Mr Allen, the chief engineer, had told her when they left Japan three days earlier. He had promised that his crew would work the engines harder than they ever had before, to get her to San Francisco on time. But what could mere men do against the ferocious rage of the Pacific?

DAY 67 — PACIFIC OCEAN For the first time in a fortnight, Nellie felt the tension in her body begin to ease. They had survived the storms, and the captain had announced that they would be in San Francisco tomorrow. What a relief! What joy! What —

With a look of horror etched on his face, one of the ship's officers burst in. A vital piece of paperwork was missing! Nellie's heart plunged towards the ocean floor as the man explained that without the lost document, nobody could leave *The Oriental* at San Francisco until the next ship arrived from Japan — and that would take *two weeks*. Nellie closed her eyes as the crew began scouring the ship. Her mouth was dry. Her stomach churned more than it had at the peak of the storm.

Suddenly a cry went up: "It's here, it's here! Right under our noses all along!" Relieved laughter and smiles erupted around her, but Nellie knew she wouldn't truly relax again until she was back in New York.

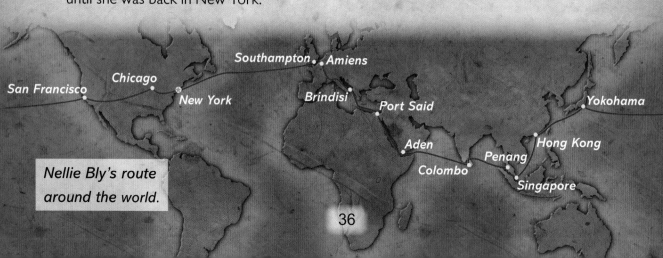

Nellie Bly's route around the world.

Homeward Bound

DAY 68 — SAN FRANCISCO, USA Nellie clutched her bag tightly as she stepped back onto American soil. She was almost 3000 miles from home and there was still plenty to worry her. Could she make it in time? Would the winter snows have blocked the railway? Where was her rival, Elizabeth Bisland?

Before she could even catch her breath, Nellie was whisked to the station. A private train, made up of a single carriage behind a powerful-looking engine, waited by the platform: clearly somebody important was in town. Eyeing it enviously, Nellie wondered who it might be for. A wealthy businessman? The President? She almost fell down when she was told it was for her! It seemed the owner of *The New York World* had spared no expense to ensure the final leg of her trip ran smoothly.

Over the next few days, crowds turned up to cheer for Nellie in every town and city the train passed through. She waved and smiled and shook hands till her arm ached. She was given so many flowers that the train soon resembled a florists' shop on wheels. She received handfuls of congratulatory telegrams — and she cried out with delight when she noticed that one of them was from Jules Verne and his wife.

Between the stops, America flashed past the windows — cities and towns, forests and farms, mountains and plains, rivers and lakes. The engine roared across the continent at record-breaking speed, bringing the finish line ever closer.

DAY 72, 3.51 PM — NEW YORK CITY She'd done it! So much for the people who said it couldn't be done! Shame on those who said no-one but a man could do it! She'd done it!

Nellie had planned to get round the world in seventy-five days. In the end, she had made it in seventy-two — a new world record. Meanwhile, Elizabeth Bisland was still crossing the Atlantic Ocean.

Cannons boomed out a salute as Nellie stepped from the train. She smiled and waved her cap to the cheering crowd, exhilarated, exhausted and, above all, very happy to be home.

Nellie's voyage made her world-famous. Her name and image soon appeared on items such as games, trading cards, pens and notebooks.

Changing Times

THROUGHOUT HER LIFE, Nellie Bly refused to be told that there were certain things women should or shouldn't do. She wasn't alone — she lived in an age where many women felt the same way.

Fighting for a Fairer World

Nellie Bly was born into a world where men and women were not equal. A woman's role was to get married, have children and then spend the rest of her life looking after her home, husband and family. Women were not expected to have ideas, opinions, careers or ambitions of their own.

Votes for Women

Until the late 19th century, no country anywhere in the world let women vote in elections to decide who ran their government. Many people — men and women — believed that women should not have opinions of their own or were unable to understand politics.

Female protesters demanding the right to vote.

© Everett Collection Historical / Alamy

© Heritage Image Partnership Ltd / Alamy

Emmeline Pankhurst under arrest in 1914.

In Britain, the campaign demanding votes for women was led by **Emmeline Pankhurst** (1858-1928). The campaigners, called suffragettes (suff-ra-jets), clashed with police during many of their protests. Emmeline was arrested several times, using each arrest to draw more attention to her cause.

In the 19th century, more and more women began to believe this was unfair. They gathered into organised groups to fight for their right to vote. Their campaigns eventually succeeded. New Zealand was the first country to give women the vote, in 1893. The USA followed in 1920, and by 1928 all women in the UK could vote. Today, almost every country in the world allows men and women equal voting rights.

Education for Women

In the early 19th century, while boys learnt maths, woodwork and technical drawing at school, girls were taught to cook and sew. It was seen as pointless to teach girls anything beyond what they needed to know to be good housewives. Many people even thought that women couldn't understand complicated subjects, and universities rarely accepted female students.

From the 1850s onwards, some teachers realised that this was unfair, and began teaching women 'male' subjects. New colleges for women were opened, and many of their students then started teaching other women and girls. In the 1860s and 1870s, some UK universities started teaching women. Today, female university students outnumber men in many countries.

Elizabeth Blackwell (1821-1910) was born in England, and moved to the USA when she was eleven. She wanted to study medicine, but she was told that women weren't intelligent enough to be doctors. However, in 1849 she became the first woman in America to gain a medical degree. She later returned to the UK and helped found Britain's first medical school for women.

Elizabeth Blackwell

Nellie Bly died in 1922. In her lifetime, the lives of women had changed dramatically. There was still a long way to go until the idea that 'a woman's place is in the home' became a thing of the past, but the pioneering women of Nellie Bly's era proved that women could succeed in areas traditionally dominated by men. In the words of Nellie's own motto:

"Energy rightly applied and directed will accomplish anything."

Glossary

asylum — A building where people judged to be insane were placed for treatment

catamaran — A type of sailing boat consisting of two narrow floating sections joined together

notorious — Having a very bad reputation

scoop — A big news story which the journalist is the first to cover

Amelia Earhart

"Queen of the skies"

written by Claire Boulter

SUMMER 1904 Amelia clumsily hammered in the last nail and stood back to survey her handiwork. The steep wooden ramp ran from the roof of the tool shed all the way to the ground.

"It was your idea, Amelia, so you should go first," said Balie, Amelia's school friend.

Amelia was only seven, but all the children in the neighbourhood looked up to her. She always had the best ideas for games, and she was never scared to try new and daring feats.

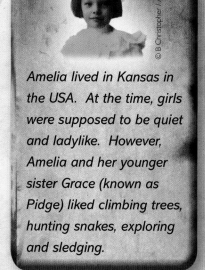

Amelia lived in Kansas in the USA. At the time, girls were supposed to be quiet and ladylike. However, Amelia and her younger sister Grace (known as Pidge) liked climbing trees, hunting snakes, exploring and sledging.

Amelia scrambled up to the roof of the shed, where her carriage — a wooden packing crate with roller skate wheels — awaited. She climbed into the box, took a deep breath, and pushed off.

The crate hurtled down the ramp, its wheels squealing in protest. It hit the ground at speed and crumpled. Amelia tumbled out. Balie and Pidge sprinted over to her limp body, their eyes wide with horror. As they peered anxiously down at her bleeding lip and torn dress, Amelia opened her eyes and grinned.

"Oh, Pidge, it's just like flying!"

While visiting a fair earlier that year, Amelia's mother told her she couldn't ride on the roller coaster. When they got home, Amelia decided to make her own.

© iStockphoto.com/Aneese

Taking Flight

WINTER 1918 Standing alone on the airfield, Amelia pulled her coat closer around her and shivered with cold and anticipation. She had been working in Toronto in Canada since the start of the year, caring for soldiers who had been wounded during the war. She had befriended lots of pilots while working at the hospital, and she was overjoyed when a group of them finally invited her to watch them fly.

The First World War lasted from 1914 to 1918. In 1918, Amelia worked as a nurse's assistant, serving meals, handing out medicine and spending time with the wounded soldiers.

She grinned and covered her ears as, one by one, the mechanics spun the propellers and the engines roared into life. The rush of air from the whirling propeller of the nearest plane blew fine, stinging snow into her eyes, making her blink and laugh. The planes lumbered heavily down the runway, then rose gracefully into the air like eagles.

Amelia was scarcely aware of time passing or of her hands gradually turning blue. She stood, frozen like a statue, as the planes soared and spiralled and swooped above her.

TWO YEARS LATER Amelia's hands shook slightly as she strapped herself into the cockpit of the plane. Behind her she could hear the pilot, Frank Hawks, settling himself in his seat. Since seeing the Canadian pilots' display, she hadn't been able to get the thought of flying out of her head. She had begged them to take her up, but she was a **civilian** and rules were rules... Her quest to take to the air had finally led her to this dusty airstrip in California.

Amelia saw her first plane at a fair when she was 10. It was a very basic machine and she dismissed it as "not at all interesting."

The pilot tapped her shoulder and gave her a thumbs-up, then began to guide the plane gently along the runway. Amelia gasped as the plane lifted off the ground.

As the ground dropped away, the trees and buildings became models on a miniature railway; the people were ants rushing busily around. Amelia's heart soared.

"As soon as we left the ground I knew I myself had to fly."

A Perfect Partnership

JANUARY 1921   Amelia jumped off the bus and set off purposefully towards the distant airfield. As she neared the bumpy, weed-infested patch of dust, she spotted a slender figure tinkering with a plane engine. Neta Snook was a successful pilot, flying instructor and businesswoman; Amelia felt a little in awe. Neta turned and greeted her, and Amelia took a deep breath.

Her carefully prepared speech flew from her mind and she blurted out, "I want to learn to fly... Will you teach me?"

Amelia did several jobs to pay for her flying lessons, including driving a truck and working for a telephone company.

"Sure," Neta smiled. "The rate's a dollar a minute. Hop in. We can start right now."

How to Fly an Aeroplane

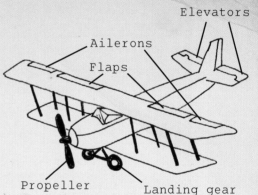

Taking off:
1. Face your aircraft into the wind. Run the engine at full power and allow it to travel forwards.
2. When you have travelled a short distance, raise the elevators to prevent the aircraft taking off. Keep them in this position until you have reached full speed.
3. Once you are up to speed, gently lower the elevators. The plane will start to lift into the air.

In the air:
1. Gain height quickly, but at a shallow angle. Aim to achieve a height of at least 800 feet.
2. Turn the plane using the ailerons. Raise the right aileron to turn right and the left aileron to turn left.

Landing:
1. When fairly close to your landing place, shut off the engine, angle the nose downwards and face the plane directly into the wind.
2. At about fifty feet above the ground, level off the plane's angle.
3. As the wheels touch the ground, raise the wing flaps to slow the plane. When the plane has slowed down, **taxi** to the hangar.

A Bird in Flight

JULY 1921 Amelia woke with a smile from a dream of flying, free as a bird. With a start, she remembered that it was her twenty-fourth birthday! Leaping out of bed, she threw on her flying outfit — old riding trousers and a leather jacket — and raced down the stairs and into the kitchen.

"Happy Birthday, darling!" Her mother kissed her cheek and placed a heaped plate of food on the table, motioning Amelia to sit down. "Now, I know how hard you've worked over the last few months, and I know you don't have quite enough yet to buy that plane you've got your eye on. So Pidge and I have decided that we're going to make up the difference. You can have your plane today!"

Speechless, Amelia turned and wrapped her arms around her mother.

OCTOBER 1922 High above the earth, Amelia circled, watching the cotton-wool clouds drift silently past. She was too high to make out the people below. The world was a patchwork of golden cornfields and emerald forests. A sapphire river snaked its way towards the distant sea.

Her body was relaxed, her mind focused solely on controlling the plane. As she rose higher and higher, her eyes flicked repeatedly to the **altimeter** on the control panel. 13 000 feet... 13 500... 13 900... just a little further... 14 000! Amelia let out a whoop. She had done it — she had broken her first flying record. She had flown higher than any other woman in the world.

Gliding gently towards the ground, Amelia smiled to herself. Now she just had to fly higher, further, faster than the men.

Neta and Amelia with Amelia's first plane. It was bright yellow, so she nicknamed it 'The Canary'.

Challenges and Opportunities

APRIL 1928 Amelia was at work, surrounded by a group of laughing, chattering children. With her mind fixed on the game the children were playing, she wasn't aware of the phone ringing until she heard a child's voice at her elbow.

"Phone for you, Miss Earhart."

Extracting herself from the crush of children, Amelia picked up the receiver. A deep voice greeted her.

*From 1925, Amelia was a social worker in Boston. She worked with **immigrant** children from poor backgrounds, planning activities and classes.*

"Miss Earhart? This is Captain Hilton Railey of the U.S. Army. I need a woman willing to fly across the Atlantic Ocean. It'll be hard work, and quite possibly dangerous. I hear you might be the woman for the job. What do you say?"

Amelia clutched the phone tighter. No woman had ever flown across the Atlantic; this was her chance to prove herself! Her heart thumping, she managed just one word: "Yes!"

JUNE 1928 Emerging from the cramped cockpit of the *Friendship*, Amelia looked around her at the lush greenness of Wales. After nearly twenty-one hours in the plane, after enduring strong winds and dense clouds, after nearly running out of fuel, they had made it.

She was the first woman to cross the Atlantic in a plane, but her pride was mingled with frustration. Far from flying the plane, her only duty had been to keep the **flight log**. Apparently, a woman couldn't be trusted with the challenging job of piloting.

When would people start to realise that women were just as capable as men? As the cheering crowds surrounded her and the rest of the crew, Amelia resolved that she would prove it, once and for all.

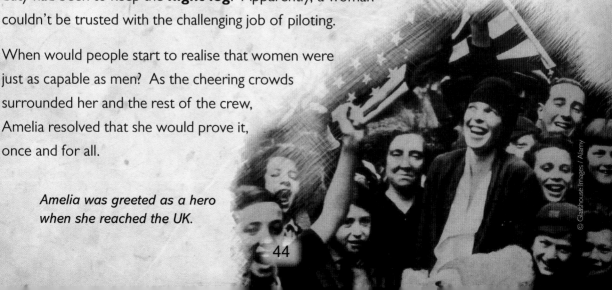

Amelia was greeted as a hero when she reached the UK.

MARCH 1929 Amelia looked up as her secretary entered the room with another pile of letters. Since returning from her transatlantic flight, she had been swamped with fan mail, requests to give lectures and write magazine articles, and even marriage proposals! It seemed that the whole world wanted to hear about her adventure.

Amelia often received more than 200 letters a day. She had a secretary to help her, but she tried to answer all the letters from children personally.

Not only that, but women were suddenly copying her style and several companies had already asked whether they could use her name on their women's clothing and luggage ranges. Amelia had agreed — on the condition that she could help design the clothes. She was delighted to see women abandoning the confining corsets and long, restrictive dresses of the past, and starting to wear trousers and shorter skirts. Finally, women were able to dress comfortably and move as freely as men.

A Brush with Disaster

AUGUST 1929 Amelia sat calmly in her new plane, feeling the power of the machine as it vibrated gently, eager to take off. This was the final leg of the first Women's Air Derby, a race of about 2700 miles across the USA. The rules were simple: the first pilot to reach the finish line won. Amelia's friend, Ruth Nichols, was also racing. Today would decide which of them was the better pilot.

Ruth was next in line to take off, and Amelia gave her a quick thumbs-up as the starter signalled for her to go. A brief roar and Ruth was off, speeding down the runway. Amelia's smile suddenly vanished. Something was wrong. Ruth's plane was slowing down, lurching sideways. The world stood still as the plane clipped a tractor parked at the end of the runway. It somersaulted, smashed into the ground and crumpled.

Before she knew what she was doing, Amelia was out of her plane and sprinting. She slowed as she reached the mangled mass of metal, ringed by shards of splintered glass.

"Ruth?" she called, her voice shaking. She heard a groan — Ruth was alive! In minutes, Amelia had hauled her friend out of the wreckage. Ruth leaned heavily on Amelia as they stumbled towards safety.

"Amelia!" Ruth suddenly stopped. "What are you doing? You were supposed to take off right after me. Get back in that plane and get going!"

Amelia laughed. She might not win this race, but there were more important things in life.

Amelia came third in the race. Later that year, Amelia, Ruth and ninety-seven other female pilots founded 'The Ninety-Nines' — an organisation that educated women about flying and provided support for female flyers.

Some of the contestants in the 1929 Women's Air Derby. Amelia is fourth from the right.

© Aircraft Collection / Alamy

Going it Alone

20TH MAY 1932 Settling herself in the cockpit, Amelia called to her advisor, "Hey, Eddie, **telegraph** George for me, would you? Just let him know I got away safely."

She wished she felt as confident as she sounded. Ever since her transatlantic flight, Amelia had longed to prove that she could make the journey solo. Finally, her chance had come. Whether she would succeed, only time would tell.

As she coasted down the runway and felt the familiar jolt as the wheels left the ground, her spirits lifted. If she made it, she would have achieved something that no other woman — and only one man — had done before.

*In 1931, Amelia married her **publicist**, George Putnam. At the time, women were expected just to look after the home and obey their husbands. Amelia refused to do this. She kept her own name and called her marriage a 'partnership' with 'dual control'.*

CULMORE CHRONICLE

Saturday May 21st 1932   One Penny

TRIUMPH FOR AMERICA'S QUEEN OF THE AIR

AMELIA EARHART HAS become the first woman to fly solo across the Atlantic.

Miss Earhart set off from Canada yesterday evening. She was aiming for Paris, but bad weather and mechanical issues forced her to end her journey in Northern Ireland.

AWFUL CONDITIONS
The trip was uneventful at first. However, four hours in, trouble threatened when the plane flew into a storm and was blown off course.

National treasure: Miss Earhart.

Next, the exhaust tubing split, so fumes started to leak out and catch fire.

The final setback came when a build-up of ice on the wings sent the plane into a downward spin. Luckily, Miss Earhart regained control just in time to save herself from a watery grave.

UNPLANNED LANDING
After 14 hours 54 minutes in the air, in a damaged plane, with fog closing in, Miss Earhart finally spotted land. With no airfield nearby, she settled for a field.

Farmhand Danny McCallion saw her land. "I approached the plane and asked her, 'Have you come far?' and when she said, 'From America,' I was stunned!"

A Brave New World

DECEMBER 1935 Sitting cross-legged on the floor, Amelia gazed at the eager faces of the young women around her. She had been working as a part-time lecturer and careers advisor at Purdue University for the past few months, and many of the students had become her friends. These evening gatherings had become commonplace, a chance for the students to quiz Amelia about her life, and to seek her advice about their own futures.

Purdue University in Indiana was unusual for the time — it had lots of female students, who were given practical training in mechanics and engineering and encouraged to pursue careers in these fields.

"But do you really think we can do the same jobs as men?" a mousy-haired girl near the back of the room asked timidly.

"I don't just think it," Amelia replied, "I know it. There's no reason why women shouldn't be engineers, scientists, doctors… whatever they want to be. We're just as smart as men, just as capable. Why shouldn't we all, men and women, have the same opportunities?"

"I have known girls who should be tinkering with mechanical things instead of making dresses, and boys who would do better at cooking than engineering."

The girl's eyes turned dreamy for a moment as she pictured a glittering career for herself. Amelia smiled; with her encouragement, these young women were beginning to see that their futures didn't have to revolve around husbands and homes.

"Anyway," Amelia stood and stretched, "I'm off to bed. I've got an early start in the morning. The university president wants to see me first thing. Apparently he has some good news."

Amelia had an inkling of what the news might be; she just hoped she was right.

Amelia with a group of Purdue University students.

48

MARCH 1936 Amelia paced around the aeroplane factory with an engineer.

"Something big," she said eagerly, as the engineer took notes, "bigger than I've flown before. And with two motors, rather than just one. Most importantly, I need extra space for fuel. Let's see how far I can get without stopping."

Three months ago, Edward Elliott, Purdue University's president, had told her that the university and private donors had raised enough money to buy her a new plane, bigger and better than anything she had flown before. Equipped with all the latest instruments so she could gather data, it would be a kind of flying laboratory. In it, she would be able to push the boundaries of flight and find out exactly what it was possible to do in a plane.

Very few people, and no women, had flown around the world before.

Planning the features of the new plane had planted a seed in Amelia's mind, which was now in full bloom: she wanted to fly around the world.

FEBRUARY 1937 Amelia, her navigator and her advisors clustered around a huge map, peering intently at endless lists of angles, dates and numbers. Amelia's planned route took her right round the middle of the globe — a total of 29 000 miles with around thirty stops.

The planning was well underway, but there were so many questions to consider. Where should she end each leg of the journey? How much fuel would she need to get there? Was the weather likely to allow her to land and take off? The list was never-ending.

"Of course, the view of the stars is somewhat limited from inside the plane, but I'll still be able to pinpoint our location with great accuracy." Fred Noonan, her navigator, paused and gave her a sudden, infectious grin. Smiling back at him, she felt a bubble of excitement rise in her chest. Soon, the long months of preparation would be over. The adventure could finally begin.

Amelia and Fred Noonan.

© Bettmann/CORBIS

Into the Unknown

MARCH 1937 So far, so good. Amelia had successfully flown 2400 miles — the first leg of her round-the-world trip. She checked the instruments one last time, called to Fred to check that he was ready and, revving the engine, started to move down the runway.

The plane skimmed effortlessly along the smooth concrete, its nose thrusting upwards, eager to take to the air. Suddenly, it swerved to the right, its wing scraping along the ground like fingernails on a blackboard. Amelia heaved the plane to the left, fighting to straighten it. It veered wildly round, its right wing crunching into the ground as it tipped. She heard the sound of screeching metal as something tore off the bottom. Finally, the plane ground to a halt. Stumbling down from the cockpit, Amelia gulped as she saw her beautiful bird lying broken on the runway, its wings shattered and flightless.

Nobody knows for sure what caused the plane to crash, but Amelia believed that it might have been a burst tyre.

1ST JUNE 1937 The first light of dawn was beginning to soften the darkness as Amelia strode down the runway towards the waiting crowd. Gazing ahead at her plane, she smiled. The Lockheed factory had done a wonderful job of fixing the damage, and the plane was as good as new. Because of the crash, Amelia and Fred had been forced to replan their whole route to avoid bad weather. Amelia sighed as she thought back over the hours of planning, the endless maps and charts and figures. At last, they were ready to try again.

Scrambling into the plane, Amelia blew her husband a kiss and waved to the crowd. She took a deep breath. This time, she told herself, everything would go better.

Start point

Amelia's planned route around the world, showing some of her stops.

Howland Island

2ND JULY 1937 In the radio room of the US Coast Guard ship, the *Itasca*, the captain and officers waited anxiously. They had been moored off Howland Island for several days, standing by to guide Amelia to this tiny pinprick in the vastness of the Pacific.

She should be arriving at Howland any time now, but for the past hour they had heard nothing. Leo Bellarts, the ship's chief radioman, clutched his microphone and tried to reach her for what felt like the hundredth time. Why wasn't she answering?

The radio suddenly crackled into life. Amelia's voice echoed strongly round the room. "Calling *Itasca*. We must be on you but cannot see you, but gas is running low."

"Go ahead," Leo replied. If she kept talking, they might be able to get a **bearing** on the plane and guide her down. The minutes dragged by with no response.

"We are circling but cannot hear you." Amelia's voice burst out, loud in the quiet room. Leo flicked frantically between **frequencies**, trying to make a connection.

"We are **running north and south**." Amelia's voice was fainter now.

The tropical sun floated lazily across the sky, but Leo was unaware of its progress as he tried, time and time again, to make contact with Amelia. There was only silence.

What Became of Amelia Earhart?

Amelia Earhart, Fred Noonan and the plane they were in disappeared somewhere over the Pacific Ocean on the morning of 2nd July 1937. They had completed more than three-quarters of their round-the-world flight. For seventeen days, the US Navy and Coast Guard scoured the ocean for hundreds of miles around Howland Island, but no trace of Amelia, Fred or the plane was found. There are several theories about what happened after the plane lost radio contact.

Lost at Sea

Many people believe that Fred's navigation was slightly out and he and Amelia missed Howland Island, ran out of fuel and had to crash-land the plane in the ocean. The heavy plane would have sunk quickly, and the water in the area is more than 5000 metres deep. This would explain why no trace of the plane or its crew was found.

Lae
Howland Island
— Planned route
- - - Possible route taken

If Fred's course was even a fraction out when the plane left Lae, they could easily have missed Howland.

Stranded

Another theory is that Amelia sighted land, and landed on an uninhabited island. One place she might have landed is Gardner Island, four hundred miles south-east of Howland. This island is surrounded by a coral reef, where a plane could safely land at low tide.

In 1940, human bones were found on Gardner Island. Analysis showed that they probably belonged to a white woman who was approximately 1.7 m tall (roughly Amelia's height).

Taken Prisoner

Some people believe that Amelia may have landed in a Japanese-occupied area. At the time, the US and Japan had a hostile relationship, and Amelia may have been taken prisoner by Japanese soldiers. A witness claimed to have seen a plane landing on the island of Saipan (Sy-pan) in 1937, flown by an American woman with short hair. However, despite extensive searches of the island, no other evidence was found that Amelia had been there.

Amelia may have ended up in a Japanese jail, suspected of being an American spy.

Despite ongoing interest, the question of what happened to Amelia remains unanswered. Perhaps one day we will learn the truth about this extraordinary woman.

Glossary

altimeter — An instrument that measures how high above sea level an object is

bearing — The direction from one object to another

civilian — Someone who isn't in the armed forces

flight log — A record of a flight

frequencies — Different channels on which radio signals are broadcast

immigrant — Someone who has moved from one country to another

publicist — Someone who promotes another person's work

running north and south — Nobody is sure what this means, but it probably means that Amelia was flying first north, then south, trying to spot Howland Island

taxi — Move along the ground on wheels

telegraph — In the past, a way of sending messages over long distances